GARFIELD
Classics

MY FIRST CLASSIC COLLECTION
CONTAINS:

THE GREAT LOVER

WHY DO YOU HATE MONDAYS?

DOES POOKY NEED YOU?

JIM DAVIS

First published by Ravette Publishing 1998

Printed and bound in Great Britain
for Ravette Publishing Limited,
Unit 3, Tristar Centre,
Star Road, Partridge Green,
West Sussex RH13 8RA
by Cox & Wyman Ltd, Reading, Berkshire

ISBN 1 85304 970 0

Garfield
The Great Lover

JIM DAVIS

ЯR

© 1982 United Feature Syndicate Inc

© 1982 United Feature Syndicate, Inc

© 1982 United Feature Syndicate inc

© 1982 United Feature Syndicate, Inc   1-20

© 1982 United Feature Syndicate Inc

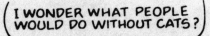

JIM DAVIS   11-10

© 1981 United Feature Syndicate, Inc

9-29

© 1981 United Feature Syndicate, Inc.

© 1981 United Feature Syndicate, Inc.

© 1981 United Feature Syndicate, Inc.

JIM DAVIS 7-31

IN THE FLOWER GARDEN AGAIN, GARFIELD?

HOW'D YOU GUESS?

© 1981 United Feature Syndicate, Inc.

© 1981 United Feature Syndicate, Inc.

ROWRR!!

HOP   HOP

JIM DAVIS   6-25

© 1981 United Feature Syndicate, Inc.

OH, GARFIELD

JIM DAVIS

5-6

© 1981 United Feature Syndicate, Inc.

© 1980 United Feature Syndicate, Inc.

4-14

JIM DAVIS

12-15   © 1981 United Feature Syndicate, Inc.

12-14

© 1981 United Feature Syndicate, Inc.

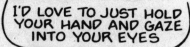

© 1981 United Feature Syndicate, Inc.

IS THIS WHERE MY CAT AUDITIONS FOR THE CAT FOOD COMMERCIAL?

YEH

8-27   JIM DAVIS

HEY, LARRY. BREAK OUT THE WIDE-ANGLE LENS

IF I DON'T GET THE PART, THE DIRECTOR IS GOING TO BE SPORTING THOSE SHADES UP HIS RIGHT NOSTRIL

© 1981 United Feature Syndicate, Inc.

© 1981 United Feature Syndicate, Inc.   8-29

TAPPITY
TAPPITY
TAPPITY

3-27

OKAY...
WHO WAXED
THE FENCH?

© 1981 United Feature Syndicate, Inc.

© 1981 United Feature Syndicate, Inc.

© 1981 United Feature Syndicate, Inc.

© 1980 United Feature Syndicate, Inc.

© 1981 United Feature Syndicate, Inc.

12-8

Garfield
Why Do You Hate Mondays?

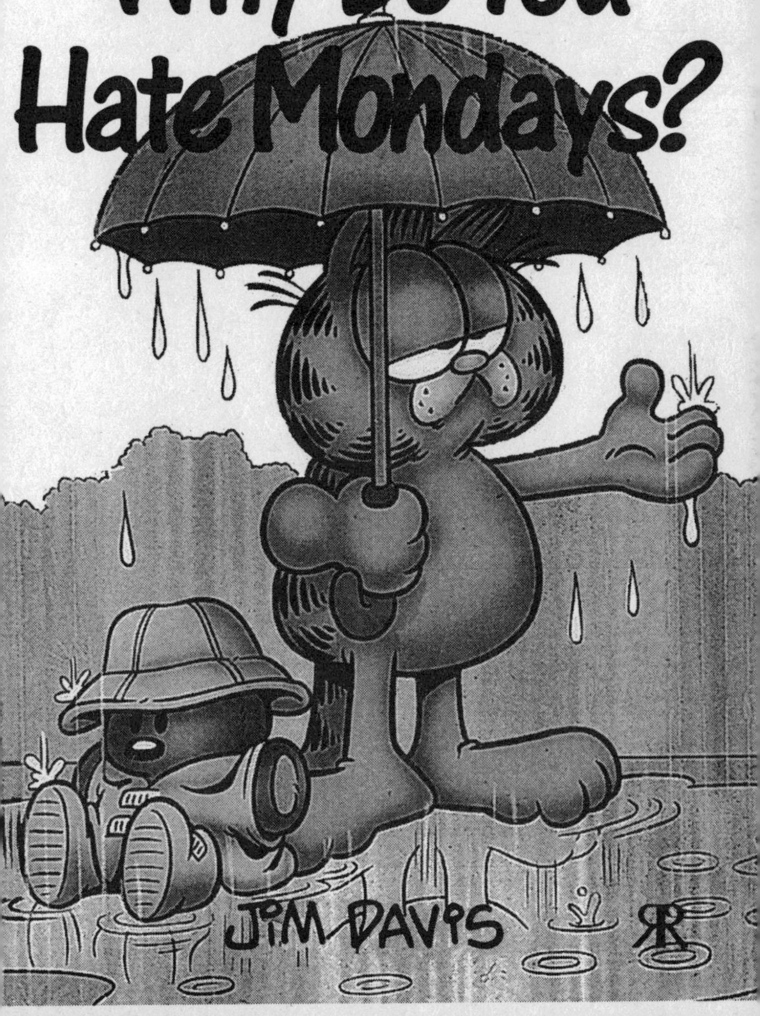

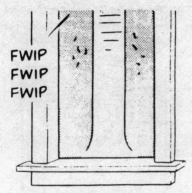

JIM DAVIS

SWIPE!

I HATE MONDAYS

© 1981 United Feature Syndicate, Inc.

JIM DAVIS

© 1981 United Feature Syndicate, Inc.

OKAY, GARFIELD. ONE BITE

JIM DAVIS

© 1982 United Feature Syndicate, Inc.

2-26

© 1982 United Feature Syndicate, Inc

SMACK!
SLURP!

JIM DAVIS   3-5

YOU HAVE THE MANNERS
OF A PIG, GARFIELD.
SLOW DOWN AND
SPIT OUT THE SEEDS

RATA TATA
TATA TATA

© 1982 United Feature Syndicate, Inc.

© 1982 United Feature Syndicate, Inc.

JIM DAVIS

© 1982 United Feature Syndicate, Inc.

BOING BOING

JIM DAVIS

HA HA, AREN'T YOU CUTE! HERE, HAVE SOME FOOD

1-4-82

I HATE MYSELF WHEN I DO THAT

© 1981 United Feature Syndicate, Inc.

JIM DAVIS

© 1981 United Feature Syndicate, Inc.

I'M GOING TO START YOU ON YOUR DIET SLOWLY, GARFIELD

JIM DAVIS 7-22

FOR THE REST OF THE WEEK YOU MAY HAVE NO DESSERTS

FINE AND DANDY

HELLOOOO, MAIN COURSE

© 1981 United Feature Syndicate, Inc.

7-25   JIM DAVIS

THE LOST-YOUR-WILL-TO-LIVE
PHASE OF THE DIET, HUH?

LET ME
DIE IN
PEACE

© 1981 United Feature Syndicate, Inc.

7-15

JIM DAVIS

BASH!

© 1981 United Feature Syndicate, Inc

7-16

GOOD MORNING, FATSO

ALL I DID WAS JUMP OFF THE BED

CRASH

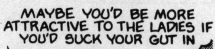

OKAY, WHO PUT
EYEBALLS ON MY
HAMBURGER?

GARFIELD, I WOULDN'T SAY YOU'RE FAT...

JIM DAVIS

BUT YOU HAVE MORE CHINS THAN A HONG KONG TELEPHONE DIRECTORY!

2-10

8-13

8-15

1-22 © 1981 United Feature Syndicate, Inc

1-23

2-3

WHAT'S SO SPECIAL ABOUT A PET-OWNER RELATIONSHIP, GARFIELD?

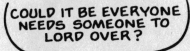

COULD IT BE EVERYONE NEEDS SOMEONE TO LORD OVER?

COULD BE

© 1981 United Feature Syndicate, Inc. JIM DAVIS

BUT WHAT DO YOU GET OUT OF IT?

11-13

JIM DAVIS   3-15

© 1982 United Feature Syndicate, Inc.

2-13 JIM DAVIS

SORRY ABOUT THAT

© 1981 United Feature Syndicate, Inc.

© 1981 United Feature Syndicate, Inc.

Garfield

Does Pooky Need You?

JIM DAVIS

11-25

OH NO!

JIM DAVIS © 1980 United Feature Syndicate, Inc.

GARFIELD, I'VE BEEN THINKING...

I'M SERIOUSLY CONSIDERING HAVING YOU DECLAWED

WHATEVER FOR?

12-9

© 1980 United Feature Syndicate, Inc.

© 1980 United Fecture Syndicate, Inc.

12·3

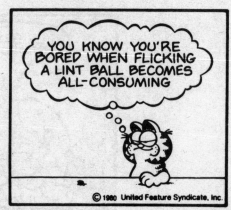

© 1980 United Feature Syndicate, Inc.

SOMEHOW, I PREFER GARFIELD IN HIS LESS AFFECTIONATE MOODS

© 1980 United Feature Syndicate, Inc.

12-8

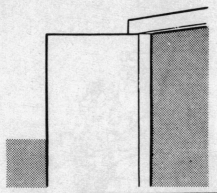

12-23

© 1980 United Feature Syndicate, Inc.

© 1980 United Feature Syndicate, Inc.

11-28

OH NO! THEY'VE RAISED MY ELECTRIC BILL AGAIN! WHAT'LL I DO?

THERE'S ONLY ONE THING TO DO IN A CASE LIKE THIS...

JIM DAVIS

12-27

SLEEP ON IT!

A REAL MAN OF ACTION

ZZZZ

© 1981 United Feature Syndicate, Inc.

© 1981 United Feature Syndicate, Inc.

© 1981 United Feature Syndicate, Inc.

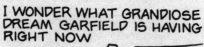

I WONDER WHAT GRANDIOSE DREAM GARFIELD IS HAVING RIGHT NOW

© 1982 United Feature Syndicate, Inc.

JIM DAVIS

7-16

JIM DAVIS

© 1982 United Feature Syndicate, Inc.

© 1982 United Feature Syndicate, Inc.

© 1982 United Feature Syndicate, Inc.

© 1982 United Feature Syndicate, Inc.

© 1982 United Feature Syndicate, Inc.

ARRRGH!

YOU'RE SUPPOSED TO BE ON MY SIDE!

© 1982 United Feature Syndicate, Inc.

© 1982 United Feature Syndicate, Inc.

© 1982 United Feature Syndicate, Inc.

© 1962 United Feature Syndicate, Inc.

JIM DAVIS

6-2

© 1982 United Feature Syndicate, Inc.

© 1982 United Feature Syndicate, Inc.

© 1982 United Feature Syndicate, Inc.

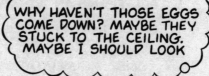

7-22

© 1982 United Feature Syndicate, Inc.

I LOVE IT WHEN YOU CUDDLE UP TO ME, GARFIELD

WHAT A WARM AND WONDERFUL GESTURE

MY NOSE WAS WET

THEN, ONCE THE POTATO IS DUG UP, IT IS SLICED, DEEP-FRIED, SALTED AND BAGGED. VOILÀ, YOU HAVE YOUR POTATO CHIP

I HATE KNOWING WHERE FOOD COMES FROM...

© 1982 United Feature Syndicate, Inc.

JIM DAVIS 5-6

ALL THE MAGIC IS GONE

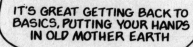

6-17

© 1982 United Feature Syndicate, Inc.

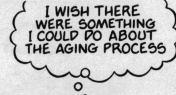

6-15

GARFIELD'S LAW: CATS ARE NATURALLY ATTRACTED TO ONLY ONE TYPE OF HUMAN BEING...

JIM DAVIS

© 1982 United Feature Syndicate, Inc.

THE TYPE WHO IS ALLERGIC TO CATS

WAHCHOO!

© 1982 United Feature Syndicate, Inc.

GARFIELD'S LAW:
CATS SHED IN DIRECT
PROPORTION TO THEIR
CONTRAST WITH A
PERSON'S SUIT

JIM DAVIS   11-15

GARFIELD'S LAW:
CATS INSTINCTIVELY KNOW
THE PRECISE MOMENT THEIR
OWNERS WILL AWAKE...

JIM DAVIS

© 1982 United Feature Syndicate, Inc.

11-10

THEN THEY AWAKEN THEM
TEN MINUTES SOONER

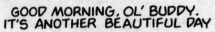

© 1982 United Feature Syndicate, Inc.

© 1982 United Feature Syndicate, Inc.

© 1982 United Feature Syndicate, Inc.

© 1982 United Feature Syndicate, Inc.

FWEEE

OTHER GARFIELD BOOKS AVAILABLE

Theme Books @ £3.99 each		ISBN
Behaving Badly		1 85304 892 5
Healthy Living		1 85304 972 7
Insults		1 85304 895 X
Pigging Out		1 85304 893 3
Romance		1 85304 894 1
Successful Living		1 85304 973 5

Classics @ £4.99 each		
Volume Two		1 85304 970 0

Miscellaneous		
Garfield Treasury	£9.99	1 85304 975 1
Garfield Address & Birthday Book Gift Set	£7.99	1 85304 918 2
	inc VAT	

All Garfield books are available at your local bookshop or from the address below. Just tick the titles required and send the form with your remittance to:-

B.B.C.S., P.O. BOX 941, HULL, NORTH HUMBERSIDE HU1 3YQ
24 Hour Telephone Credit Card Line 01482 224626
Prices and availability are subject to change without notice.

Please enclose a cheque or postal order made payable to B.B.C.S. to the value of the cover price of the book and allow the following for postage and packing:

U.K. & B.F.P.O:	£1.00 for the first book and 50p for each additional book to a maximum of £3.50.
Overseas & Eire	£2.00 for the first book, £1.00 for the second and 50p for each additional book.

BLOCK CAPITALS PLEASE

Name ....

Address..

....

....

Cards accepted: Mastercard and Visa

☐☐☐☐☐☐☐☐☐☐☐☐☐☐☐☐

Expiry Date ....Signature ....